After a degree in English Literature at Cambridge, Keith Ravenscroft had a career as a writer and creative director in international advertising agencies. He moved gradually from atheism to faith in mid-life and is now an Anglican Lay Minister which involves teaching, preaching and leading worship. Keith has lived in Canada and Italy in the past, and his passions are music, philosophy, theology and Christian spirituality as expressed in poetry and mystical writings. Keith is married to Avril, who is a graphic artist and an Anglican Priest. They have four children and three grandchildren.

I'm dedicating this book to my daughter, Chloe, who first suggested that I might be able to keep in contact with the residents of Care Homes, even when we couldn't meet in person. Without her encouragement this book would probably not have been written. I'd especially like to thank the residents and staff contacts of two local care homes: The Beaumont in Prestbury, and Belong at Upton Priory for their enthusiasm and feedback. I also have a debt to Reverends Sue Hawkins and Rob Green for their support and insights. And as always I owe a massive thank you to my dear wife, Avril, who made valuable suggestions as to Bible texts and subjects.

Keith Ravenscroft

# UNFORGOTTEN

Reflections on Loss,
Loneliness and Love

AUSTIN MACAULEY PUBLISHERS™
LONDON • CAMBRIDGE • NEW YORK • SHARJAH

A CIP catalogue record for this title is available from the British
Library.

ISBN 9781035804399 (Paperback)
ISBN 9781035804405 (Hardback)
ISBN 9781035804429 (ePub e-book)
ISBN 9781035804412 (Audiobook)

www.austinmacauley.co.uk

First Published 2024
Austin Macauley Publishers Ltd®
1 Canada Square
Canary Wharf
London
E14 5AA

# Introduction

This book of Reflections is meant for anyone who has ever felt, and maybe still feels today, lonely, excluded, even abandoned. Or for anyone who knows or identifies with someone in that situation. It's a state of mind and heart that brings suffering to so many people. My intention is to support anyone who feels this way with some messages of comfort and hope.

After the loneliness of lockdown which has massively increased those feelings, this is a crucial time to stay in touch with ourselves, each other, and with God. Lockdown has demonstrated to us, powerfully and painfully, how we as humans rely on each other to maintain our sense of self, and if we are people of faith, above all to maintain our faith and closeness to God.

This series of brief reflections was originally designed to support those residents of two local care homes that before the pandemic I used to visit and regularly taken Communion to. As this was no longer a possibility I framed these thoughts as a way of, as our church described our mission then, 'being together though apart'. I was relieved to find that these regular communications were welcome, but surprised and delighted that other people I knew seemed to relate to them just as personally.

Now that the worst of the pandemic seems to be over, at least at the time of writing, it is increasingly clear that it has left its mark on all of us. And that therefore some continuing form of support and encouragement might be welcome now and in the future. For that reason, I have adapted the reflections I've written over the past few years (and which I continue to write and deliver to care homes regularly) and combined them into this book.

I haven't attempted any dense theologising or learned biblical interpretation. I feel that more people may react positively to one direct and simple thought that can encourage them and maybe even clarify for them that though we have lost a lot that is not recoverable through the pandemic, what we have *not* lost is of even greater value. We can still discover with new urgency that God is as close and as caring as ever. That we are still as much a part of one another and of Him as we could ever hope to be. And that even in our worst moments of stress and loneliness we are 'Unforgotten' by God. Because our names are *written on the palm of his hand*, and we remain 'his people and the sheep of his pasture', now and for all eternity.

These reflections do not follow a chronological sequence. Each one is complete in itself and therefore can be read in any order, depending on whether a particular issue resonates with you on a particular day. That is very much the way I wrote them, as issues and Bible texts came to the forefront of my mind. Many were written at the height of the pandemic, and I have left in references to those times. I hope that you will get from these reflections some of the same hope and comfort that came to me as I wrote them.

I'd like to thank the residents and staff of my local Beaumont and Belong Care Homes for their enthusiasm for this project, and their feedback. Most of all I thank my wife Avril for her insights and support, and my dear daughter Chloe who suggested this scheme to me in the first place. Without her prompting I would not have had the impetus to embark on it.

Keith Ravenscroft
June 2022

# Reflections

# 1. A Message of Hope and Trust

In these troubled times we all need to remain safe and strong. And this is a time when our faith can help us the most. Here is God's faithful promise to us from Isaiah—chapter 43. Let the healing words soak into you for a while:

**'Do not fear, for I have redeemed you;**
**I have called you by name, you are mine.**
**When you pass through the waters, I will be with you; and through the rivers, they shall not overwhelm you; when you walk through fire you shall not be burned, and the flame shall not consume you. For I am the Lord your God, The Holy One of Israel, your Saviour…**
**You are precious in my sight, and I love you…**
**Do not fear, for I am with you.'**

Even at this time of threat and uncertainty, though it can be hard sometimes not to feel alone and isolated, we can still take comfort and strength from the unending and ever-faithful love of God, expressed in so many ways and through so many voices in the Bible. Over the months from now on I plan to share some of these messages with you regularly…

Isaiah was speaking to people who like us could feel dispossessed and often disorientated. Everything they had held onto seemed shaken to its foundations, as they were cast into exile from their homes and had lost the familiar support of friends and family. The words of comfort and care spoken by God were a rallying cry to them then, and they are just as much of one to us now! 'Do not fear... I have called you by name, you are mine.'

We wait, as the Israelites waited, for better times. And they will return. All bad things will come to an end. And the good things that come from God will remain, infinite and everlasting. So for this let us pray, together though apart:

**Heavenly Father, we thank you for your loving care and for the comfort of your holy Word. For reminding us that each one of us is precious in your sight and that you love us and are always here beside us way beyond our imagination or understanding.**

**Keep us safe and strong, patient and kind, to ourselves as well as to others. As we wait for the better days that will surely come. These things we ask in the name and for the sake of our Lord and Saviour Jesus Christ.**

**Amen.**

# 2. Acts of Kindness and of Love

People say that it takes a crisis for us to realise what matters most in life, and what is trivial. I have found that the crisis we have been suffering from in the Covid-19 pandemic has brought out the best in people in very noticeable ways. The small and unexpected kindnesses, sometimes from the most unlikely people, the recognition that we are creatures who depend on each other. The importance of relationships and community at a time of forced isolation. All these things have caused us to rethink and reprioritise who and what we care about the most. We find ourselves in a world that may in many ways seem alien and strange, but one that is also filled with what Wordsworth in one of his loveliest poems described as:

**'Those    little,    nameless,    unremembered    acts Of kindness and of love.'**
**(From 'Tintern Abbey')**

Small these acts may be, but precious they are too. And they do not go unremembered either! They reflect the love of God for all his people, and they let us be witnesses to the world of that love.

Wherever we look in the Bible we will find no more fervent and tender expression of God's love for us than in the lines below. As we are told how by expressing, sharing, and living love in our own lives 'God lives in us, and his love is perfected in us.'

**Beloved, let us love one another, because love is from God; everyone who loves is born of God and knows God. Whoever does not love does not know God, for God is love. God's love was revealed among us in this way: God sent his only Son into the world so that we might live through him. In this is love, not that we loved God but that he loved us and sent his Son to be the atoning sacrifice for our sins. Beloved, since God loved us so much, we also ought to love one another. No one has ever seen God; if we love one another, God lives in us, and his love is perfected in us.**

**(The First Letter of John—chapter 4, verses 7–12)**

These are words that lighten our burden, bring us good news in times of trouble (or joy). Holy words that are worth savouring and holding close, as they stress the importance of love for one another.

Some people claim that God sends bad things to us either as punishment or to jolt us into dread of him. I believe such a belief is a tragic mistake. More than that, it is almost blasphemous to claim that God's will for us is punishment as well as love. What I do believe is that God is capable of bringing good out of even the worst of the human predicament. The outpouring of kindness that has emerged even from Covid-19 pandemic is proof of that. It is a gift for which we may all feel strengthened and thankful.

So let us pray, together though apart:

Loving Father of all people, we thank you for your love for us, and we vow to spread it to each other in our lives and in your name. Rejoicing that human goodness will always triumph over what is evil. Because every act of kindness and of love is a small example of the endless goodness and mercy that comes from your infinite power and love.

Amen.

# 3. All the 'Wrong' People are Invited into the Kingdom of Heaven

'Go away from me Lord, for I am a sinful man!' That's the desperate cry from Simon Peter who as a fallible ordinary person, not unlike you and me, finds himself in contact with the absolute power, absolute goodness, and inescapable call of Jesus to travel with him and to be his own. It is a call that can be hard to answer, because it makes everything else seem insignificant. So Simon Peter protests, tries to hide from the call, but is borne along by his awareness of something greater than he can understand.

Of all the disciples I think Peter is the one we know best and identify with the strongest. I can imagine myself feeling as he did and saying what he said:

**Once while Jesus was standing beside the lake of Gennesaret, and the crowd was pressing in on him to hear the word of God, he saw two boats there at the shore of the lake; the fishermen had gone out of them and were washing their nets. He got into one of the boats, the one belonging to Simon, and asked him to put out a little way from the shore. Then he sat down and taught the crowds**

from the boat. When he had finished speaking, he said to Simon, 'Put out into the deep water and let down your nets for a catch.'

Simon answered, 'Master, we have worked all night long but have caught nothing. Yet if you say so, I will let down the nets. When they had done this, they caught so many fish that their nets were beginning to break. So they signalled to their partners in the other boat to come and help them. And they came and filled both boats, so that they began to sink. But when Simon Peter saw it, he fell down at Jesus 'knees, saying, 'Go away from me, Lord, for I am a sinful man!' 'For he and all who were with him were amazed at the catch of fish that they had taken; and so also were James and John, sons of Zebedee, who were partners with Simon.'

Then Jesus said to Simon, 'Do not be afraid; from now on you will be catching people.' 'When they had brought their boats to shore, they left everything and followed him.'

(Luke's Gospel—chapter 5, verses 1–11)

Jesus calls us not for what we are or have been but for what we are capable of becoming under His guidance and in the power of His love. That is how God's Salvation works upon all of us, if like Peter, we will welcome God into our lives. Throughout the Gospels we see this self-confessed '*sinful man*' being brave, being cowardly, coming to profound insights yet so often missing the point. Just as we do. Until Peter answers Jesus' probing question right at the end of John's Gospel: 'Lord, you know everything. You know that I love you.' And then all questions are answered, all hurts healed. As they will be, by the grace of God, in our own lives!

So let us pray, together though apart:

**Lord who knows everything, and knows us more fully than we know ourselves. Bring us to knowledge of you, and faith in you, despite our many human failings. So that we may grow under your guidance and flourish in the warmth of your love.**

**Amen.**

# 4. The Promise
# of Better Times to Come

Isaiah knew what it was like to feel lost, to be separated from all that he held dear. In exile with the Israelites as if imprisoned in the land of Babylon, far from home. But Isaiah had a message of hope to share with his people. 'Help is coming. The Lord is coming. All that is wrong will be put right. All that is lost will be returned to us.' Here are some of the words of faith and encouragement that we hear sung year upon year in Handel's Messiah. About the Good Shepherd who will feed his flock and lead them into safety. As at this time of Advent we realise that Isaiah is foretelling the world-changing arrival of our Saviour Jesus Christ.

**He will feed his flock like a shepherd. He will gather the lambs in his arms and carry them in his bosom... those who wait for the Lord shall renew their strength, they shall mount up with wings like eagles, they shall run and not be weary, they shall walk and not faint... I will turn the darkness before them into light, the rough places into level ground.**

**(Isaiah—chapter 40, verses 11–31, chapter 42, verse 16)**

It is to Isaiah that we can turn for comfort in our own time of trouble, as we face this seemingly endless imprisonment that we suffer because of the virus. Our faithful God will, like a good shepherd, turn the darkness before us into light and turn the rough places where we stumble into level ground again.

Thanks to the amazing skills of science, and God's eternal loving care, we can finally look forward to better times. When we shall be reunited with our loved ones who we miss and who miss us so much. Able once again to share, and to embrace. So let us look forward to that day, as we pray, together though apart:

**Jesus Christ, Son of God, good shepherd of your flock,**
**Be with us today and every day. Strengthen, encourage, and comfort us with your loving presence in this time of isolation. Help us to wait in faith and trust for better times, knowing that those who wait for the Lord shall renew their strength. And bring us through Advent to the joyful Christmas time when the whole Christian world comes together to remember your birth among us.**

**Amen.**

# 5. The God Who Will Never Forsake Us

In troubled times like these we need more than ever the reassurance of God's presence and love as we wrestle with the challenges that life has thrown at us. These regular messages from me, with quotes, reflection, and a prayer, are designed to remind you that you are not alone. Not on those silent and solitary days. Not ever. No matter what may come to test you. Here is a promise for us from St Paul.

**'Who will separate us from the love of Christ? Will hardship, or distress, or persecution, or famine, or nakedness, or peril, or sword… No, in all these things we are more than conquerors through him who loved us. For I am convinced that neither death, nor life, nor angels, nor rulers, nor things present, nor things to come, nor powers, nor height, nor depth, nor anything else in all Creation, will be able to separate us from the love of God in Christ Jesus our Lord.'**

**(Paul's Letter to the Romans, chapter 8, verses 35–39)**

This is an impassioned cry of faith and hope from Saint Paul, as he wrestles to come to terms with his own sufferings in the service of Christ, and to comprehend fully the meaning of Christ's death and Resurrection. Because of the overwhelming challenges of Paul's ministry that will finally lead to his death in Rome, we might expect his words to be full of fear or self-pity. But not one bit. Instead Paul voices his concern and offers his reassurance to all his followers, declaring his unwavering belief that he, and they, and we, are all enfolded together in the eternal love of Jesus Christ who paid the ultimate sacrifice out of the depth of his undying love for us. These words still resonate with us in our times of trial these two thousand years later. Because they are meant not just for that moment long ago, but for the strengthening of all people in all times and places.

Our lives are full of trial, and never more so than today, in this time of lockdown and separation from those people we love and who love us. Hard as it is, we can and must hold onto these words of promise, for they apply to all those who feel locked away and lonely in their care homes. As we allow Paul's promise to sink into our hearts, to light up our prayers, and to strengthen our bonds with those we still can meet each day, his words tell us of the light at the end of the tunnel that will surely make all clear again. And of the love of Christ, who walks every step with us, however dark the road may seem today.

So let us pray, together though apart.


**Lord Jesus, shed the light of your everlasting love on the darkness of these days. Be with us when things are at their toughest, and keep us secure in faith and hope. Reassure us that we are never alone and never outside your tender care. Fill us with faith and hope, so that like your servant Paul we may witness to your presence in**

every place and every situation. Lord, hold us up, support us, be with us in all our prayers and contemplation and in our impatience too. As we wait for the better times that will surely come again.

Amen.

# 6. 'I Am the Bread of Life This Is the Bread That Comes Down from Heaven.'

When we are hungry and thirsty the need for food and drink blocks out all other sensations. But there is another even greater kind of hunger that we may all have felt at one time or another. The hunger to understand what our lives are about. And it is that hunger and thirst for God that Jesus is talking about.

Jesus so often spoke in metaphors and this one, that he is 'the bread of life' is the most frequent and for me the most powerful. Imagine if we lived, as the people of Israel did in Jesus' day, and as so many still do in our world today, in a society where lack of basics was always a fear and a cloud over daily life. For those people who heard Jesus his words would have had an urgency that we can only imagine. And yet our hunger for that 'Bread of life' is just as strong now. Which is why the Christian message has retained its relevance and its power right up to today. Read and savour Jesus' words and you'll feel that power for yourself:

**Jesus said to them, 'I am the bread of life. Whoever comes to me will never be hungry, and whoever believes**

in me will never be thirsty… This is indeed the will of my Father, that all who see the Son and believe in him may have eternal life; and I will raise them up on the last day.'
'I am the living bread that came down from Heaven. Whoever eats of this bread will live forever; and the bread that I will give for the life of the world is my flesh.' Because of Jesus' words (that they could not understand) many of his disciples turned back and no longer went about with him. So Jesus asked the twelve, 'Do you also wish to go away?'
'Simon Peter answered him, 'Lord, to whom can we go? You have the words of eternal life. We have come to believe and know that you are the Holy One of God.' (John—chapter 6. Between verse 35 and the end of the chapter)

'You have the words of eternal life' says Peter. 'You are the Holy One of God.' Let us echo Peter's words, and give thanks that we are blessed with the love of Jesus, who is and (who shares with us during our Communion services) 'the living bread that came down from Heaven.' As we pray now, together though apart:

**Heavenly Father, we thank you that we are never abandoned and alone. That you are always with us, and that whatever happens in our lives, its joys and sorrows, and all its challenges, we are fed with the bread of eternal life, received from your blessed hand at the moment of Holy Communion.**

**Amen.**

# 7. 'You Did Not Choose Me but I Chose You'

I heard about a Bible scholar from Germany who went to teach in a college in the USA. With his halting and heavily accented English he must have seemed to come from another planet. When asked to give their opinion of him one of the students replied:

**'We're not sure we understand him, but we're absolutely sure he understands us.'**

In the final conversation that Jesus has with his disciples before his arrest, often known as The Long Goodbye, he says so much that is hard for them to understand totally. But what they do realise is his love and care for them even as he approaches his moment of greatest suffering. In the passage below from John's Gospel the words that spring out for me are 'You did not choose me, but I chose you'. Here is the God who created us and all things welcoming us as his friends, sharing with us all that he is and all that he wants for our wellbeing and salvation. As we bear the fruits of faith in him and show it by loving each other:

'This is my commandment, that you love one another as I have loved you. No one has greater love than this, to lay down one's life for one's friends. You are my friends if you do what I command you. I do not call you servants any longer, because the servant does not know what the master is doing; but I have called you friends, because I have made known to you everything that I have heard from my Father. You did not choose me but I chose you. And I appointed you to go and bear fruit, fruit that will last, so that the Father will give you whatever you ask him in my name. I am giving you these commands so that you may love one another.'

Even when we may find it hard to understand and believe in Jesus he always does and always will understand and believe in us. As Isaiah tells us, God has 'written our name on the palms of his hand from all eternity'. May that love compel us to respond with love to him and to each other. As we are commanded to do in what Jesus called *the first and greatest* of those Ten Commandments. To love God and our neighbour. As God has loved us.

So let us pray, together though apart.

**Lord of life and love, who chooses us to be his beloved friends, help us to trust and believe in you, even when life brings us challenges to our faith and understanding. Certain that you know who we are and what we need, even when we ourselves may not know.**

**Amen.**

# 8. 'Death Has Been Swallowed Up in Victory'

I'm writing this when the joy of Easter Sunday is still fresh in my memory. Inevitably that freshness tends to fade over the year, and the full significance of Jesus' Resurrection risks becoming a distant historical event rather than an ever-present living reality. The full meaning of Easter Resurrection is of course exactly that. A living, world-changing reality, then and now.

In defeating death and returning to full life Jesus heralded a revolution in our understanding of the meaning and possibility of human life itself. Jesus has triumphed over death not just for himself but for all of us. In the extract from Paul's Letter that I quote below, Paul explains the full force, the revolutionary difference, of what Jesus has caused to happen.

We now know that our life here on Earth is not the beginning and end of human destiny but simply the end of the beginning. And that what awaits us, through God's grace and love, is a future that stretches way beyond our earthly end into an infinity of eternal life and joy in God's presence. We can feel the certainty and triumph in Paul's words as if we were hearing him speaking directly to us. As of course he is, which is why his words have survived these two thousand years and are among the most loved and revered of all passages in the Bible. Let the forceful, confident love of what he says work on you now:

**Behold, I will tell you a mystery! We will not all die, but we will all be changed, in a moment, in the twinkling of an eye, at the last trumpet. For the trumpet will sound, and the dead will be raised imperishable, and we will be changed. For this perishable body must put on imperishability, and this mortal body must put on immortality. Then the saying that is written will be fulfilled:**

**'Death has been swallowed up in victory.' 'Where, O death, is your victory?**

**Where, O death, is your sting?'**

**Thanks be to God, who gives us the victory through our Lord.**

**Jesus Christ—First Letter to the Corinthians, chapter 15, verses 50–57**

Christ's Resurrection means that our own resurrection is something we can hope for and look forward to with joy! That is the continuing, everlasting significance of Easter, the fullest expression of God's love for us. So let us 'give thanks to God, who gives us the victory through our Lord Jesus Christ':

Heavenly Father, we thank you for the sacrifice and victory of your dear Son at Easter. Help us to keep in our hearts that His victory is our victory too, and to look forward to the joyful life in His eternal presence that you have prepared for us.

Amen.

# 9. 'Do You Love Me?'

If there is one thing that can actually be harder than being offered forgiveness it is to find the strength to forgive ourselves in return. So often we carry a heavy but unnecessary burden, when we could come to terms with the pains and failures of the past and make a joyful new start. Instead of which we live imprisoned in the loneliness of guilt.

Our Christian faith is one that believes in fresh starts, in the realisation that what we have been and what we are can be transformed through divine forgiveness into what God aches for us to be. All we have to do is ask and accept and we can be transformed into a new self, living a new life.

In the reading I've chosen we find Simon Peter in just that quandary. He has been the most vocal, the most forthright, and it would seem the most courageous of Jesus' disciples, yet he of all people has denied that he even knew Jesus, for fear that what was happening to Jesus could happen to him as well. All his hot headiness has frozen into cold fear. And now he has to confront the risen Christ. He would expect a reproachful, searching gaze from the man who he called Lord. Who he betrayed and then, stricken with guilt, *went out and wept bitterly.*

But instead of blame and anger Peter is greeted by Jesus with a gentle, searching and repeated question: 'Simon, son of John, do you love me?' Baffled, desperate, and confused, Peter struggles to convince his Lord with escalating desperation, finally blurting out:

'Lord, you know everything. You know that I love you.'

And Jesus, the One who knows everything and forgives everything, entrusts Peter to continue his own work. *'Feed my sheep.'* Peter is to be transformed, given the courage to speak out for Jesus, to convert multitudes, and ultimately to share his Lord's death:

**When they had finished breakfast, Jesus said to Simon Peter, 'Simon son of John, do you love me more than these? 'He said to him, 'Yes, Lord; you know that I love you.**

**'Jesus said to him, 'Feed my lambs. 'A second time he said to him, 'Simon son of John, do you love me? 'He said to him, 'Yes, Lord; you know that I love you.'**

**Jesus said to him, 'Tend my sheep. He said to him the third time, Simon son of John, do you love me? Peter felt hurt because he said to him the third time, Do you love me?' And he said to him, 'Lord, you know everything; you know that I love you.'**

**Jesus said to him, 'Feed my sheep. Very truly, I tell you, when you were younger, you used to fasten your own belt and to go wherever you wished. But when you grow old, you will stretch out your hands, and someone else will fasten a belt around you and take you where you do not wish to go.' (He said this to indicate the kind of death by which he would glorify God.) After this he said to him, Follow me.'**

So let us leave our guilts and our regrets at the foot of the Cross and accept the new start that God offers us. As we pray, together though apart:

**Heavenly Father, may we too learn to accept God's forgiveness and then learn to forgive ourselves for our past mistakes and failings. So that, strengthened and transformed, we may follow you our Maker and Redeemer, saved and protected within the loving care of our Good Shepherd.**

**Amen.**

# 10. Lent: Let's Make It a Time for More Not Less

What does Lent mean for you? For many Christians it means having less, doing less. Self-denial. In memory and imitation of Jesus who, despite being aware of his limitless divine power, denied himself the power to change his fate when tempted to do so in the desert. But by doing so offered us more, not less, as he launched his ministry.

**Jesus, full of the Holy Spirit, returned from the Jordan and was led by the Spirit in the wilderness, where for forty days he was tempted by the devil. He ate nothing at all during those days, and when they were over, he was famished. The devil said to him, 'If you are the Son of God, command this stone to become a loaf of bread. 'Jesus answered him, It is written, One does not live by bread alone.'**

**Then the devil led him up and showed him in an instant all the kingdoms of the world. And the devil said to him, 'To you I will give their glory and all this authority; for it has been given over to me, and I give it to anyone I please.' If you, then, will worship me, it will all be yours. 'Jesus answered him, It is written, worship the Lord your God, and serve only him.'**

**Then the devil took him to Jerusalem, and placed him on the pinnacle of the temple, saying to him, 'If you are the Son of God, throw yourself down from here, for it is written, "He will command his angels concerning you, to protect you."**

**"On their hands they will bear you up, so that you will not dash your foot against a stone." Jesus answered him, It is said, "Do not put the Lord your God to the test." When the devil had finished every test, he departed from him until an opportune time.**

Lent can be a very challenging time for us at the best of times, but especially now at what has been and is still being, for now at least, through lockdown, the worst of times. That's why I want to suggest that this year of all years must have already felt like a year-long Lent of involuntary self-denial. And for that reason, maybe Lent for us this year could be a time when God may want us to be more than usually gentle on ourselves. To accept in gratitude those small blessings that may seem to have been withheld from us for so long. And to pass them on to the people we know, as our Lenten gift to God.

I'm not arguing for thoughtless self-indulgence. But looking forward at this time of isolation to the long-withheld presence of loving family or friends. So maybe this Lent will bring us the freedom to mingle, to communicate, to smile when we may not feel like smiling. Any freedom of any kind! Not least the freedom to do something positive, however small.

Speaking of things positive, I once met some people from a church near Birmingham who were saying that they didn't give up things for Lent. Instead they tried to do things that they didn't normally do. I asked them for an example, and was amused—and then moved—by the reply:

'We try to say something nice about somebody—behind their back.'

I think those people understood better than most of us what Lent is about. So let us pray, together though apart:

**May God teach us during this time of Lent how to be gentle with ourselves, to explore not just the limits of our own self-control, but to bear witness also to the limitless scope of your love and to be witnesses to it. Spreading that love as best we can to those we meet, live with, work with, or simply love. And let that be our sacrifice of praise for Lent. For the sake of Jesus Christ, our loving Redeemer.**

**Amen.**

# 11. 'To See the World in a Grain of Sand And Eternity in an Hour'

I was talking to my sister yesterday and she reminded me of how we used to collect conkers together, when we were little children. Instantly I was taken back over many years to be again the small boy I was then. Back to the smell of wet leaves, frosty grass sometimes, the shock of horse chestnuts spilling out from green shells. A world that was vast and magical, and a small child living within the wonder of it all.

In the face of God's Creation, we are all small and wondering. The quotation above from a poem by William Blake sums it up powerfully. He saw behind appearances into the deep down reality of things. And in the Book of Genesis we are shown the moment of Creation in all its freshness and beauty, the wonder of everything as it emerges from nothing by the will of God:

**"And God said 'Let there be light' and there was light."**

Many of the most famous religious thinkers, including the great St Augustine, have described Nature as God's second Bible that is there to be read as the word of God.

This coming Sunday we celebrate Harvest Festival, also known as Creation Sunday. It's a time to remember, to re-experience, and to give thanks for all the wonders that surround us. To look around and to see afresh the beauty of our world. To love and protect it. And in my case to remember that the little boy rooting around for conkers is the same person who today is still 'small and wondering' and thankful when I'm confronted by the majesty of God's Creation. As in the words of that lovely hymn:

*'For the beauty of the earth,*
*For the beauty of the skies,*
*For the love that from our birth*
*Over and around us lies,*
*Father, unto thee we raise*
*This our sacrifice of praise.'*

So let us give thanks to God for our world, together though apart:

**Heavenly Father, thank you for showing and sharing with us the gift of your Creation, speaking as it does of your majesty and love. Fill our senses with Nature's beauty, help us to protect what we have been given. And may the world around us be for us a foretaste of your eternal Kingdom where joy and beauty will reign forever.**

**Amen.**

# 12. 'Surely Goodness and Mercy Shall Follow Me All the Days of My Life'

If people were asked to vote on which passage from the Bible is most loved and quoted, Psalm 23 would certainly be near the top of the list. It has that unique ability to express thanks, trust, confidence, and praise in God's goodness and mercy throughout all human life, and beyond into eternity. As that lovely hymn puts it:

*Through all the changing scenes of life,*
*In trouble and in joy,*
*The praises of my God shall still*
*My heart and tongue employ.*

And nowhere does that praise ring out more wholeheartedly than here. The Psalm Chapters are often described as the prayer book of the Old Testament. Some of these prayers are desperate and full of grief, as the 'changing scenes of life' assail them, but this Psalm Chapter above all is confident in its thanks and joy. Some three thousand years ago, maybe even longer, this psalm was being sung by pilgrims on their way to give thanks at the Temple:

**Psalm 23**

The Lord is my shepherd; I shall not want.

He makes me to lie down in green pastures: he leads me beside the still waters.

He restores my soul: he leads me in the paths of righteousness for his name's sake.

Yea, though I walk through the valley of the shadow of death, I will fear no evil: for thou art with me; thy rod and thy staff they comfort me.

Thou preparest a table before me in the presence of mine enemies: thou anointest my head with oil; my cup runneth over.

Surely goodness and mercy shall follow me all the days of my life: and I will dwell in the house of the Lord for ever.

That trust shining out in the midst of life's challenges and inevitable griefs speaks to us as strongly now as way back then. And in the New Testament, Jesus describes his people (and we are his people, now as then) as sheep without a shepherd, and himself as the Good Shepherd who protects and saves, and lays down his life for the sheep.

So whether our lives lead us through green pastures and beside still waters, or through the storms and turmoil that no human life can escape, God's goodness and mercy is all encompassing. And beyond it is the promise that we shall 'dwell in the house of the Lord for ever'. Some three thousand years later and for all eternity we too, like the writer of this healing, calming, psalm, are held close and secure in the everlasting love and care of the eternal God. So let us pray, together though apart:

Heavenly Father, we thank you that you are with us and for us through all the changing scenes of life. We bring to you our thanks, our troubles, and our joys. And we pray that when our lives on Earth are done we may 'dwell in the house of the Lord forever'.

Amen.

# 13. 'Out of His Anguish He Shall See Light'. And so, Shall We.

It always astonishes and saddens me that so many people celebrate Easter Sunday in church but are nowhere to be seen on Good Friday. They are keen to be there for the pleasure but prefer to avoid the pain. Surely though that is to miss the point about Easter and actually about life itself. Let me explain what I mean.

To understand and appreciate joy we need to know what grief is. We know that, I'm certain, from our personal lives. We appreciate the light more intensely when we emerge from darkness. And darkness and light are exactly what Easter is about. It is only by walking the dark road to Calvary with Jesus in spirit that we can fully share the burst of light that Easter morning brings. 'Out of his anguish he shall see light' as Isaiah prophesied in the sequence that has become known as 'The Suffering Servant'. This passage seems to foretell the Crucifixion and Resurrection of Jesus. When we have followed him through the darkness of Calvary, we shall share that light with him. After the tragedy, the triumph! We get a glimpse of what that change must have felt like in Luke's account of Jesus meeting pilgrims on the road to Emmaus. He turns their despair at the Crucifixion into celebration of his

Resurrection before their eyes. As he first reveals the meaning of the scriptures and then reveals his risen self to them:

**'Oh, how foolish you are, and how slow of heart to believe all that the prophets have declared! Was it not necessary that the Messiah should suffer these things and then enter into his glory?' Then beginning with Moses and all the prophets, he interpreted to them the things about himself in all the scriptures.**

**As they came near the village to which they were going, he walked ahead as if he were going on. But they urged him strongly, saying, 'Stay with us, because it is almost evening and the day is now nearly over. So he went in to stay with them. When he was at the table with them, he took bread, blessed and broke it, and gave it to them. Then their eyes were opened, and they recognised him; and he vanished from their sight.' They said to each other, 'We're not our hearts burning within us while he was talking to us on the road, while he was opening the scriptures to us?' 'That same hour they got up and returned to Jerusalem; and they found the eleven and their companions gathered together. They were saying, 'The Lord has risen indeed, and he has appeared to Simon! Then they told what had happened on the road, and how he had been made known to them in the breaking of the bread.'**

'Out of his anguish he shall see light.' Let us pray that by walking through the darkness of Calvary together on Good Friday we may then see the light, the dazzling burst of joy that is Easter Morning:

Heavenly Father, we thank you for the story of our Salvation, which we hear as we share the loneliness of Christ's Cross each Easter. Show us the light of your love for us, and strengthen us to follow you, our faithful friend, more faithfully.

Amen.

# 14. Even the Greatest Grief Can Be Transformed into Joy.

**She said to them 'They have taken away my Lord, and I do not know where they have laid him… Jesus said to her, Woman why are you weeping? For whom are you looking?…**

**Then Jesus said to her, "Mary!" She turned and said to him in Hebrew,**

**"Rabbouni"**

**which means Teacher.'**

**(John 20:13–16)**

Easter Sunday is the dawn of a whole new world. For the grieving Mary, for us who have waited throughout Lent and shared the loneliness and pain of Good Friday. And for the whole world. Nothing will ever be the same again for those of faith. Mary has come grieving, yet bravely, faithfully alone, to find the dead Jesus in his tomb and minister to him for one final time. Braving the darkness of night, and the darkness in her own soul. But to her horror the tomb is empty. Convulsed with sorrow, she cannot understand what has happened. Who could? But soon she will. Jesus has broken the bonds of death. The public shame and horror of Calvary now gives way to a never imagined reunion in the sweet morning air and blessed privacy of a garden. As the risen Jesus reveals himself for the first time, not to the rich and powerful, not to men who control life in this ancient society, but to a lonely desperate woman. His beloved Mary.

The saying that things are at their very darkest in the hour before dawn has never been more true than in this moment. Until the onrush of joy banishes all else. 'He is risen indeed!' as Christians say triumphantly each Easter Sunday. And this Easter Sunday, as each year, at my church of St. Peter's, shadowy figures will congregate in the churchyard in the light of just a flickering log fire. Then as dawn arrives, they will take a lighted brand and process into the church, light the Easter Candle, and in joy and thankfulness, celebrate together the first Communion of Easter.

Just as we can only be with Mary in Spirit on that holy morning, may we all be together as well—in Spirit at least—in the church that we most love. In my case the ancient church of St Peter's. As we share the joy of resurrection to new life that is as fresh as that first morning in the garden, and new *every* morning! And as we contemplate this gift from God, let us pray, together though still apart.

**Dear Lord, risen Saviour and faithful friend, we thank you for the great sacrifice you made for us, and we share the joy of your victory over death, knowing that you have promised us also a share in eternal life in your Kingdom. Keep us strong, keep us faithful, fill us with hope, even when the darkness can seem never ending, and the light so far from our grasp. As Easter morning dawns and we join with our fellow Christians throughout the world to exclaim 'He is risen indeed!'**
**Amen.**

# 15. A Time of Personal Revaluation. Who Can We Be in the Eyes of God?

Lent has come around again, a time of serious reflection. A time to review who we are and where we are in the eyes of God. A time to repent (a word which originally meant to 'change direction'). An opportunity to reset our compass as it were. But importantly Lent should not be experienced as a time of despair at the great gulf between who we are, even the best of us, and who we could and should be, but rather as a time of hope for positive change.

We remember the temptations of Jesus in the desert, but today I want to think about a very human story from much earlier in the Bible, and which is equally suitable for this time of Lent. It comes way back in the Book of Genesis. It's the story of the repentance of Jacob.

Jacob became one of the fathers of the nation of Israel, after a dramatic conversion experience. Before that he had been a con man who cheated his brother Esau of his birthright by tricking their blind old father Esau. A man whose way of living was one of double dealing. And in the passage below Jacob has been fleeing from the revenge of his brother Esau, and is terrified to death of what Esau will do to him when they now have to meet.

And then God intervenes, Jacob is forced to come clean about who he is before he can confront Esau in honesty. He repents and becomes a different person. Here is the moment that changes everything:

**Jacob was left alone; and a man wrestled with him until daybreak. When the man saw that he did not prevail against Jacob, he struck him on the hip socket; and Jacob's hip was put out of joint as he wrestled with him. Then he said, 'Let me go, for the day is breaking.' But Jacob said, 'I will not let you go, unless you bless me.'**

**So he said to him, 'What is your name?'**

**And he said, 'Jacob.'**

**Then the man said, 'You shall no longer be called Jacob, but Israel, for you have striven with God and with humans, and have prevailed.'**

**Then Jacob asked him, 'Please tell me your name.' But he said, 'Why is it that you ask my name?' And there he blessed him. So Jacob called the place Peniel, saying, 'For I have seen God face to face, and yet my life is preserved.' 'The sun rose upon him as he passed Penuel, limping because of his hip.'**

**(Genesis—chapter 32, verses 24–31)**

What this story of Jacob demonstrates is that it is never too late to change. And that God's blessing is always available, just waiting for us to want it. And that, good or bad, strong or weak, we are all beloved by God. Our Lenten time of repentance for what we have been, and our hope for what we may become, is unlikely to be as dramatic or as necessary as what happened to Jacob. But the story reminds us, as we confront this testing time of Lent, that we are all beloved by God. And that just as the angel blessed Jacob, God's blessing is there for every one of us. So to express our determination to let Lent work upon us, let us pray together:

**Heavenly Father, strengthen our determination to be the people you long for us to be. May this time of Lent bring us closer to you, help us to know and love you better and to strive more consistently to do your will. And shower your blessing upon all of us, as we grow in knowledge of who we are in your sight.**

**Amen.**

# 16. A New Year,
# a Timeless Promise for Us All

At a time like this, when we have just plunged into yet another lockdown, it can be hard to see the rainbow for the rain! Sometimes we can feel as if we are the only people who have ever had to face a time like this—but of course we are not. Throughout the Bible we hear God's promise that out of the worst situation he will bring renewal. That He never has and never will abandon us in our time of need. The following extracts from the Bible state God's promise powerfully, A promise that is just as faithful today as it was then. The first promise is the one we are given by Isaiah:

**'Do not remember the former things, or consider the things of old. I am about to do a new thing: now it springs forth, do you not perceive it?' (Isaiah—chapter 43, verse 19)**

As so often in the Bible, even out of the wreckage God can bring renewal. In the case of the Israelites, that meant a return to their own land, the end of their painful exile in Babylon. For us it can mean the prospect of the end of our own exile from all that makes life sweet, because of the complexities and constraints of having to struggle through this pandemic.

God's same promise is repeated even more powerfully in the sending of Jesus as a light to a world plunged in darkness, as we have so recently celebrated this past Christmas. And at the end of the Book of Revelation, in that mystical vision in which the Second Coming of Christ in glory heralds a future of eternal bliss for the whole world. There the 'new thing' described so long before by Isaiah now comes to its eternal fruition:

**'Mourning and crying and pain will be no more, for the first things have passed away... See, I am making all things new.' (Revelation—chapter 21, verses 4–5)**

My hope is that although these words cannot make the pandemic and its problems go away, they may give us a perspective that makes them that little bit easier to bear. So let us pray, together though apart:

**Heavenly Father, help us to feel your presence with us at our time of need. Give us the patience to endure what must be endured. And shine the light of your peace upon us today and every day. In the name and in the strength of your beloved Son, Jesus Christ.**

**Amen.**

# 17. 'Joy Comes with the Morning'

Even when everything around has seemed gloomy, as if we were stranded in some endless night, we know that morning will come again. Now thankfully we are seeing the first precious rays of light with the arrival of the vaccines. That hope and confidence has never been more needed and precious than in this time of pandemic with the darkness of seemingly endless lockdown having been around us for so long. It can be so hard to be patient, to keep our spirits up, to trust, although we know that the power of scientific ingenuity will finally change our lives for the better.

Life is never uncomplicated and human beings like us have been in such situations from time immemorial. Sometimes they have left us with a record of their struggles and triumphs from ages long past. This feeling, and the encouragement that we can gain from it, is best summed up for me by the Psalm Chapters that have come down to us from ancient times. Ancient they may be, these personal outpourings, but they reflect how we feel today just as much as how those nameless writers and singers felt thousands of years ago on their pilgrimages of faith. Because although societies change, human feelings and longings remain the same.

I personally find the psalms act like a life raft. It's as if we cling onto them and they keep us afloat when it feels as if the waters are rising around us. They help to reassure us that, in those words of Psalm 30:

**'Weeping may linger for the night, but joy comes with the morning.'**

The psalms demonstrate many moods, and not all of them are cries of desperation and pain. Some sing out with joy, reassuring us that God's arms are always wrapped around us to protect us, hidden though they may be from us at times:

**'The Lord is my shepherd; I shall not want**… **he restores my soul… I fear no evil; for you are with me**… **Surely goodness and mercy shall follow me all the days of my life, and I shall dwell in the house of the Lord forever.'** **(from Psalm 23)**

Other psalms celebrate the God who knows precisely where we are on our journey, and who realises that we may need plucking from the darkness into the eternal light of his love. Like the psalmist in this extract we are led to marvel at this God who is always there for us:

**'Even the darkness is not dark to you, the night is as bright as the day, for darkness is as light to you.'(from Psalm 139)**

So God promises us solidarity in our sorrows and celebrations, in our doubts and in our joys. One of our best-loved hymns sums up those two extremes beautifully. I wish I could sing it to you (but knowing the limitations of my voice it may be a mercy that I can't! Maybe you can sing it for yourself instead). It begins:

*'Through all the changing scenes of life,*
*In trouble and in joy.*
*the praises of my God shall still*
*my heart and tongue employ.*
*O magnify the LORD with me,*
*exalt his name;*
*When in distress to him I called,*
*He to my rescue came.'*

That hymn describes the nature of the psalms so perfectly it seems to me. Life rafts to cling onto in time of trouble, songs of hope and celebration of God's loving kindness to help us to glory in the promise of Salvation.

So together though apart, let us give thanks that we can finally see the first light of the morning that will bring us freedom and joy, as we begin to reconnect with those we love, and reclaim the life that has been put on hold for so long:

**Heavenly Father, we bring before your loving mercy the sorrows of our long night of separation, and we look forward together to the joys of renewed life that will return to us again as morning breaks and freedom returns. And we thank you that you are always with us and for us, in all the changing scenes of life, in trouble and in joy.**

**Amen.**

# 18. 'Here Am I; Send Me'

One of the things that so often keeps people away from accepting God's love is a feeling that we are unworthy of it. That is a total misunderstanding of who God is, and it can sadly and unnecessarily get in the way of faith.

None of us is worthy of such an astounding gift, but it is on offer to all of us nonetheless. Because God doesn't keep score and give us marks out of ten, with a success or failure rate. He understands what is in our hearts, the ways in which we fall short of our best selves. God is not so much concerned with what we have been, or even what we are now. But in what we long to be. And what we can become when we are called by Him. Only He knows where our faith can take us.

If this sounds like letting ourselves off the hook too easily, it is far from that. We find throughout the Bible examples of people who felt incompetent, unready, and most of all unworthy. But who became the prophets and the witnesses, who are most celebrated in the story of Salvation.

Moses told God he couldn't possibly lead the Israelites because he was tongue-tied. Jeremiah's excuse was that he was just a child. Peter asked Jesus to 'depart from me because I am a sinful man'. And Isaiah, in one of my favourite passages in the whole of the Bible, describes himself as a man of unclean lips. And yet God has called him anyway…

In the year that King Uzziah died, I saw the Lord sitting on a throne, high and lofty; and the hem of his robe filled the temple. Seraphs were in attendance above him; each had six wings: with two they covered their faces, and with two they covered their feet, and with two they flew. And one called to another and said:

'Holy, holy, holy is the Lord of hosts; the whole Earth is full of his glory.'

The pivots on the thresholds shook at the voices of those who called, and the house filled with smoke. And I said: 'Woe is me! I am lost, for I am a man of unclean lips, and I live among a people of unclean lips; yet my eyes have seen the King, the Lord of hosts!'

Then one of the seraphs flew to me, holding a live coal that had been taken from the altar with a pair of tongs. The seraph touched my mouth with it and said: 'Now that this has touched your lips, your guilt has departed and your sin is blotted out. 'Then I heard the voice of the Lord saying, whom shall I send, and who will go for us? And I said, Here am I; send me!'

Isaiah's calling was highly dramatic. But after all the drama of the scene, Isaiah's response is simple and humble. 'Here am I. Send me.' We are all called in one way or another. It is usually gently and imperceptibly, as if the Holy Spirit whispers in our ear.

We may not even be aware of it at the time, perhaps not until years later. And most of us are not called to perform dramatic acts, or to make an impact that will change the world—though maybe, just maybe, we can have a positive effect on the people around us. By being witnesses to God's love and to the change it can make to any of us 'worthy' or not! Just as it did to those prophets of old and can still today to anyone who puts their life into the loving hands of our Lord Jesus.

So let us pray, together though apart.

**Heavenly Father, we thank you for calling all people to be your people. And that, worthy or unworthy, all are loved and valued by You. May this knowledge be life-changing for us, and may we live secure in God's love, whatever challenges life may throw at us.**

**Amen.**

# 19. 'Thy Kingdom Come, Thy Will Be Done'

'Thy Kingdom come, thy will be done... Thine be the Kingdom, the power, and the glory, forever and ever, Amen.' Christians say those words each time they recite The Lord's Prayer. We are praying for something wonderful, mysterious, eternal, to break into our lives. But what exactly is this Kingdom? Because the words are so familiar, we may no longer ask ourselves what we actually mean when we say them, which is why Jesus felt the need to tell people again and again what he meant by this mysterious 'Kingdom'. And he does so in many ways, two of which I quote here from Mark's Gospel.

Jesus describes this Kingdom in the simple terms that a farming community such as that of ancient Palestine could relate to:

**The Parable of the Growing Seed**
**He also said, 'The kingdom of God is as if someone would scatter seed on the ground, and would sleep and rise night and day, and the seed would sprout and grow, he does not know how. The earth produces of itself, first the stalk, then the head, then the full grain in the head.**
**The Parable of the Mustard Seed**

**He also said, 'With what can we compare the kingdom of God, or what parable will we use for it? It is like a mustard seed, which, when sown upon the ground, is the smallest of all the seeds on earth; yet when it is sown it grows up and becomes the greatest of all shrubs, and puts forth large branches, so that the birds of the air can make nests in its shade.'**

**With many such parables he spoke the word to them, as they were able to hear it.**

**(Mark—chapter 4, Verses 26–28, 30–33)**

But what people *'were able to hear'* was not always what Jesus meant by the Kingdom. He was talking not so much about a physical place, but a way of being. A state of mind and heart that would cause us to live in the way God intended. Something that like a growing seed ripens as if by invisible magic. That starts tiny and grows huge, like the mustard seed that grows into a mighty shrub.

So it is with the Christian life. As Jesus said at another time, 'The Kingdom of God is within you.' Every time we long and pray for the better, more just world that God intended—we shall find that with every small inward impulse and each service of love that we perform, individually or together, we help to bring that world closer. It's as if we are saying and meaning *your Kingdom come.* Because the Kingdom is the new God-given way of being that grows like a seed in our hearts.

**So let us pray, together though apart:**

**Heavenly Father, each time we pray 'yours is the Kingdom' help us to remember with gratitude that**

through your will and your grace that Kingdom can be ours also.

Amen.

# 20. Love Came
# Down at Christmas

If we ever needed to remember the power of love, it is at the end of a grim year like this has been. With its limitations on what we can do, who we can see, where we can be. And with the downright isolation and loneliness, apart from those we love most, that so many of us have had to battle against here in our care homes. So the arrival of Christmas shines a light in the darkness as it always does, but this year the light is needed even more than ever.

Like us, the shepherds in our reading were living on the margins, away from the centre of things, and yet they were the first to hear the glad news and to find a joy that they had never known. Let us hear and share their joy and amazement in these well-known and much-loved words that come from the second chapter of Luke's Gospel:

**In that region there were shepherds living in the fields, keeping watch over their flock by night. Then an angel of the Lord stood before them, and the glory of the Lord shone around them, and they were terrified. But the angel said to them, 'Do not be afraid; for see—I am bringing you good news of great joy for all the people: to you is born this day in the city of David a Saviour, who is the Messiah,**

the Lord. This will be a sign for you: you will find a child wrapped in bands of cloth and lying in a manger.' And suddenly there was with the angel a multitude of the heavenly host, praising God and saying, 'Glory to God in the highest Heaven, and on Earth peace among those whom he favours!'

When the angels had left them and gone into Heaven, the shepherds said to one another, 'Let us go now to Bethlehem and see this thing that has taken place, which the Lord has made known to us.' So they went with haste and found Mary and Joseph, and the child lying in the manger.

So *Love came down at Christmas* at that time, and so it does today. Reassuring us that we are not alone. That the greatest love that could ever be imagined is with us now, is with us always, from the God who knows us all by name and values us for who we are. Let us carry this comfort in our hearts today and always. These 'tidings of great joy' are for all people, and for us especially at a time when we need them the most!

So we pray, together though apart:

**Heavenly Father, as we welcome the coming of your Son yet again this Christmas, help us to keep faith with you as you keep faith with us. Let the Christmas story remind us of your holy presence and your support and endless love, in everything we think and do. Give us the strength and the determination to see this difficult time through, and to wait for the better times that will surely come. These things we ask in the name and for the sake of**

your dear Son Jesus Christ. Tiny child today, yet holy Lord and Saviour of all, for now and for all time.

# 21. 'Had a Lubby Day Mummy'

Our youngest little daughter happily sleepy in bed, at the end of her third birthday. Still feeling the warmth of that 'lubby' (lovely) day we had tried to give her. It's one of those moments that warm the heart of any parent. But more even than that. It's a moment when we remember that every day, every moment of every day, can and should be treasured. In a way that small children instinctively know how to do, but that we because of our adult rationalising selves seem to have lost the ability for.

**'This is the day that the Lord has made. Let us rejoice and be glad in it.'**

These words are taken from Psalm 118, often used at the opening of the service of Morning Prayer. As we wake up to new possibilities and new blessings. But also of course, inevitably, to new challenges and maybe new sorrows.

It is tempting to shrug off our natural sense of wonderment when things get tough. To become cynical to the point of despair. But these are the very moments when we may dig deep into ourselves and find comfort and strength from the God who is always with us, in bad times as well as in good times. So many poets, theologians, and songwriters have given us comfort, insight, solidarity. And hope to lean on.

So with our daughter, now a woman in her forties but still a child at heart, I wish you a 'lubby day'. Safe in the care of the one whose love is ever-present and everlasting. On good and bad days. So we pray, together though apart:

**Heavenly Father, as your beloved children we pray for the joy and the clarity of childhood to fill our hearts again. We thank you for your love and your closeness. And we hold onto hope even when life is hard. and when we may feel defeated and dispirited. Knowing that you are with us and for us, and that underneath supporting us always are your everlasting arms, whatever our lives may bring.**

**Amen.**

# 22. 'Blessed Are Those Who Mourn, for They Will Be Comforted'

(Matthew 5, Verse 4)

On this day, and on every day, so many of us carry the burden of grief that comes from the loss of dear ones, or in sharing the pain of those whose life has been blighted by long-term illness. And all of us hold in our hearts any who mourn as we try to support ourselves and each other through our darkest times.

This day, as we give thanks nationally for the saving work of Marie Curie, is about creating a bond, a circle of care, among those who mourn.

But in what way can we honestly say 'blessed are those who mourn'? And in what way will they 'be comforted'? Is it simply to underestimate the burden of grief that so many have to carry? No, just the opposite! By accepting this 'blessing' we are doing our utmost to look ahead, from the darkness of now to the light that is to come. And we are quoting the one person in the history of the world who has the greatest understanding of mourning and of the only place where comfort ultimately exists: In Jesus himself. As Isaiah described him:

**'A man of sorrows and acquainted with grief.'**

In giving us these 'Beatitudes' (these blessings) Jesus allied himself with all those whose life brings them suffering, who like him are 'acquainted with grief'. Who share the tragic sense of what it means to be human, as well as the joys that they also acknowledge and share throughout their lives. Jesus does not mean that sorrow is nothing, and nor should we. It can dominate and overwhelm all else as he above all people knew full well. And anyone who tries to diminish the hold that grief can have on us is underestimating its power.

So let us support each other in our griefs, but let us also look forward to that time when sorrow is just a memory, when the darkness will be outshone by the light of the Kingdom which is our eternal home, and where we believe that our loved ones are held safe already, living:

**'On a farther shore and in a brighter light'**

And let us take comfort in God's promise that in the end all shall be well. As Jesus said to his disciples when they grieved at the prospect of losing him: **'Now you have only sorrow: but I will see you again, and your hearts shall rejoice, and your joy on-one will take from you.' (John's Gospel—chapter 16, verse 22)**

And let us pray together for comfort and healing today, in our time of loss:

**Heavenly Father, whose Son experienced the most overwhelming sorrow that the world could throw at him, and yet was not overwhelmed, give us strength and hope**

to live through the darkness of grief and to set our hope and trust on the light of joy and glory to come. Which shall transform us, and those we love. And have lost, now but not forever.

Amen.

# 23. God Understands
# Our Inner Selves

We live in two very different worlds. The outside reality that we all share, and the inner reality of our own thoughts, beliefs, and loves—things that are personal and precious to us. Often we may not wish to, or may not even be able to, share these inner impulses with others.

These two 'selves', the public and the private, are both parts of the real 'us'. And at some special moments those two realities come together and people know us for who we really are, deep down. Maybe for the first time.

In the passage from Mark's Gospel that I'm sharing with you, Jesus experiences just such a moment, as he responds to the confusion—and indeed scepticism—of the people who think they know him. Jesus' revelation of his inner self as the Son of God is huge, our revelations about ourselves much more modest of course! But the comparison is still valid I believe.

**Jesus left that place and came to his home town, and his disciples followed him. On the sabbath he began to teach in the synagogue, and many who heard him were astounded. They said, 'Where did this man get all this? What is this wisdom that has been given to him? What**

deeds of power are being done by his hands! Is not this the carpenter, the son of Mary and brother of James and Joses and Judas and Simon, and are not his sisters here with us?' And they took offence at him. Then Jesus said to them, 'Prophets are not without honour, except in their home town, and among their own kin, and in their own house.' (Mark's Gospel—chapter 6, verses 1–4)

This first moment of Jesus' revelation of himself is God given and world-changing. Our revelation of course is nothing like on the same scale! But it comes from the power of the same God. When we disclose ourselves as Christians some people will be delighted, maybe relieved, even keen to join us. Others may resent or even mock, as they did Jesus. 'We know you; we've always known you. How come you suddenly tell us you are a part of this strange thing called 'Christian faith'?

**'Prophets are not without honour, except in their home town, and among their own kin, and in their own house.'**

That is Jesus' explanation. In a small way as Christian believers we too are prophets, the tellers of 'home truths'. We tell of a better way of living, a promise of eternity. And we gladly follow the One who shows us the way and can take us there. So one of our greatest joys is when we discover that there are people, dear to us or even unknown to us, who are prepared to walk with us on that amazing journey!

So let us pray, together though apart.

Dear Lord and Saviour, we thank you for knowing and loving our deepest selves, however ordinary our lives may seem to the outside world. And as you have loved us, so may we love and trust you in return. As part of your growing family of faith, walking together on the journey of Salvation.

Amen.

# 24. What Would It
# Have Felt Like to Be There?

One of the most amazing things about the Bible is the way it can transport us to places and introduce us to people that make the whole story of Salvation come alive for us, ever fresh. So that we are no longer isolated observers, but part of a great 'cloud of witnesses' who, like us, have responded to the drama of Salvation. One of the most dramatic moments in the whole of the New Testament is the triumphant ride into Jerusalem on what is now known as Palm Sunday, for which Jesus chooses, not a fine carriage or a white stallion, but a humble donkey.

Jesus' choice is typical of his ability to change peoples' expectations of who he is and why he has come among us. In choosing to arrive in humility upon a dusty, weary, beast of burden, Jesus has chosen to symbolise that he is no ordinary king, but 'The Servant King', who like this humble beast bears our burdens for us.

In this and so many of his acts Jesus intentionally overturned people's expectations of what God must be like. He exploded the power structures of his time and our time. The donkey's unknowing participation in the huge event of which he is a humble, furry, dusty part reminds us that we too can never, in this life at least, totally understand with our human minds what God has done by living among us in such vulnerability. So Jesus appeals directly to our human hearts. I find the symbolism very touching and I hope that it may touch you too, as we prepare for the drama of Palm Sunday. In preparation for the tragedy and triumph of Holy Week that is to follow:

**Heavenly Father, bring us to a closer understanding of what your dear Son suffered for our Salvation. Feed our imaginations, and let the story of Palm Sunday fill our hearts with humility, wonder, and love for you.**

**Amen.**

# 25. Signs of Better Times to Come

The arrival of the new vaccines gives us hope. Hope that we shall be set free from the seemingly endless lockdown that our lives have become. Thanks to human ingenuity and scientific knowledge we are witnessing the signs of change, telling us of better times to come!

The Bible story of the life and ministry of Jesus is full of signs of better times—for us, and for the whole world. Through the way Jesus was able to change the old reality into God's new one, the tediously predictable into the totally unexpected. Despair into hope. The wedding at Cana, that familiar account which you'll see below is the first of those signs in John's Gospel of a new way, a new freedom. Signs that erupted throughout his ministry, to give us a sense of God's saving presence amongst us:

**On the third day there was a wedding in Cana of Galilee, and the mother of Jesus was there. Jesus and his disciples had also been invited to the wedding. When the wine gave out, the mother of Jesus said to him, 'They have no wine.' And Jesus said to her, 'Woman, what concern is that to you and to me? My hour has not yet come.'**

**His mother said to the servants, 'Do whatever he tells you.' Now standing there were six stone water-jars for the Jewish rites of purification, each holding twenty or thirty gallons. Jesus said to them, 'Fill the jars with water.' And they filled them up to the brim. He said to them, 'Now draw some out, and take it to the chief steward.' So they took it. When the steward tasted the water that had become wine, and did not know where it came from (though the servants who had drawn the water knew), the steward called the bridegroom and said to him, 'Everyone serves the good wine first, and then the inferior wine after the guests have become drunk. But you have kept the good wine until now.' Jesus did this, the first of his signs, in Cana of Galilee, and revealed his glory; and his disciples believed in him. (John—chapter 2, verses 1–15)**

The wine had run out so the celebration could have ended in failure and shame. The tension must have been tangible. But in turning the water into wine Jesus shows that, against all the odds, he has 'kept the good wine until now,' kept the best until last. The new wine becomes a symbol for us of new life in Christ, of Salvation itself. When everything feels stale, when hope seems out of reach, the love and power of God, brought to us in Jesus Christ, is stronger than doubt or despair.

Even in the darkest hours, beset by all the problems we are going through, God promises us a future in which waiting and wondering will be no more. And for us today the new vaccine is our first sign, our new hope, our promise of better times over the horizon. So let us pray for a brighter future, together, though still apart:

Heavenly Father, world-changing Son, who brings hope out of despair and joy out of sorrow, we thank you for the signs of hope and salvation that we read about in your Holy Bible. As in our troubled times we long for the better times that will surely come. We thank you for the skill and commitment of all scientists and doctors, and of those who care for us day by day. As we wait, and hope, and trust, in your loving care. Through Jesus Christ our Lord,

Amen.

# 26. All Shall Be Saved

On the day after the attack on the Twin Towers in New York City, forever known as 9/11, a friend of mine went into her church and, on saying how frightening this event was got the reply: 'We're not frightened. We've been saved.'

It would be hard to find a statement that was so much a contradiction of everything that God stands for. Love and care for all people, in good times and bad. Not the assumption that some people are closer to God's attention than others, that they have the inside track, leaving the rest of us enviously on the sidelines. As if God's love was something we have to earn by believing all the 'right' things expressed in the right jargon.

(As a matter of interest my friend became a priest and is now a senior cleric responsible for almost 150 churches! Her care and commitment towards all God's people, 'saved' or not, is boundless and inspiring to see.)

The Bible reading below gives us God's strongest reply to those who would wish to elbow others aside, and monopolise God's loving attention for themselves. Jesus's response to James and John tells us all we need to know about God's nature and what it means to follow him in all humility, however much or little we are able to do that in our own strength.

James and John, the sons of Zebedee, came forward to him and said to him, 'Teacher, we want you to do for us whatever we ask of you.' And he said to them, 'What is it you want me to do for you?' And they said to him, 'Grant us to sit, one at your right hand and one at your left, in your glory.'

But Jesus said to them, 'You do not know what you are asking. Are you able to drink the cup that I drink, or be baptized with the baptism that I am baptized with?' They replied, 'We are able.'

Then Jesus said to them, 'The cup that I drink you will drink; and with the baptism with which I am baptized, you will be baptized; but to sit at my right hand or at my left is not mine to grant, but it is for those for whom it has been prepared.'

When the ten heard this, they began to be angry with James and John. So Jesus called them and said to them, 'You know that among the Gentiles those whom they recognize as their rulers' lord it over them, and their great ones are tyrants over them. But it is not so among you; but whoever wishes to become great among you must be your servant, and whoever wishes to be first among you must be slave of all. For the Son of Man came not to be served but to serve, and to give his life a ransom for many.'

'Jesus came to save all humanity as 'a ransom for many.' The greatest being who ever lived came 'not to be served but to serve' and was prepared to be 'slave of all.' Jesus knows us for what we have been, who we are, and who we long to be, and He loves all his fallible creatures with infallible love and mercy. He intends 'that all human beings shall be saved' as St Paul writes. Not just the favoured few! For which we can thank God, today and every day.

So let us pray, together though apart.

Loving Lord, we thank you that your love is for all time and for all people. Not just for some favoured few. Help us to understand the truth of Salvation and to grasp it with both hands, as we pray.

Amen.

# 27. And His That Gentle Voice We Hear

Next Sunday is the celebration of Pentecost, that moment when we are told in the Bible that the Holy Spirit descended on the disciples like *tongues of fire.* It enabled them to speak in tongues, a mysterious spiritual language before then unknown. And it gave them the power to witness strongly to their faith in Jesus, and to convert others to it.

It may seem like a special set of gifts, and indeed it is. But importantly it is not confined to special people. The Spirit is in all of us, the gift of God that is closer than the air we breathe. So now we have reached that point in the Bible story when Jesus has returned to his Father and we are left with the Bible account of the divine Spirit of God that from the very beginning 'moved upon the face of the waters' as described in the first lines of the Book of Genesis. Or the still small inner voice that Elijah heard after the earthquake. So after Jesus has completed his mission on Earth and returned to the Heaven from which he came we are not left alone and comfortless. The Spirit takes up residence within us. The same comforter that Jesus promised us before he left his disciples: 'The Spirit of Truth who comes from the Father, he will testify on my behalf.'

And that same Spirit lives with us and within us—all of us—here and now. There is a beautiful hymn that you will probably know. It expresses the presence and influence of the Holy Spirit in our lives more powerfully than any other words I can think of:

*'Our blessed Redeemer, ere he breathed*
*his tender last farewell,*
*a guide, a comforter, bequeathed with us to dwell.*

*He came sweet influence to impart,*
*a gracious, willing guest,*
*When he can find one humble heart wherein to rest.*

*And his that gentle voice we hear,*
*soft as the breath of even,*
*that checks each thought and calms each fear,*
*and speaks of Heaven.*

*And every virtue we possess,*
*and every conflict won,*
*And every thought of holiness,*
*are His alone.'*

May that Holy Spirit of God, the companion and comforter, live in our hearts at this time of Pentecost and always. Closer to us than the air we breathe!

Let us pray for that gift of God, together though apart:

**Heavenly Father, Son of Salvation, Spirit of comfort and truth, we thank you for the unfailing presence of your**

love in our lives, in good times and in bad. Teach us to listen for and hear that gentle voice of the Holy Spirit, soft as the breath of evening. May it calm each fear and speak to us of Heaven.

Amen.

# 28. I Am the Good Shepherd. I Know My Own and My Own Know Me.

I'm writing this in bright Spring morning sunshine. Up in the hills surrounding our town are fields full of young lambs. All ears, soft woolliness, bounding around in boundless curiosity. Nothing quite as newborn and irresistible as a lamb! So when Jesus compares us to his sheep and himself as the faithful shepherd, it tells us a lot about him—about his tender love for us and our need for him. Our need for guidance, for loving care. For direction and protection, whatever life may throw at us. No matter how much we may stray or get lost!

This picture of shepherd and sheep is one of the constant and most touching images in the Bible. The much-loved Psalm 23 reassures us that:

**'The Lord is my shepherd**
**I shall not want.**
**He makes me lie down in green pastures,**
**He leads me beside still waters,**
**He restores my soul.'**

And in John's Gospel quoted below Jesus tells us who he is, why he has come, and how he will scoop up all of us, whether we belong already in his fold or need to be guided into it.

**'I am the Good Shepherd. I know my own and my own know me, just as the Father knows me and I know the Father. And I lay down my life for the sheep. I have other sheep that do not belong to this fold. I must bring them also, and they will listen to my voice. So there will be one flock, one shepherd. For this reason the Father loves me, because I lay down my life in order to take it up again.**

**(John—chapter 10, verses 14–17***)***

After the drama of Easter, with its sorrow and then its triumph, I find it reassuring to return in our hearts to the constant, supportive presence of the Good Shepherd in our lives. May we always hold onto him, as he holds onto us from everlasting and for evermore. Whether we are already safe in his fold or not! In sure and certain hope that where he is there we shall also be!

So we pray, together though apart:

**Dear Lord Jesus, Good Shepherd of the sheep, through all the changing scenes of life, in trouble and in joy, may we hold fast to your guiding presence. Lean on you for support and feel your everlasting love.**

**Amen.**

# 29. Whoever Has Seen Me Has Seen the Father'

One of the hardest truths that Christians (and those of no faith) have to wrestle with is to understand the nature of God. The One who is not just a great Being but the ground of Being itself. The One by whose power everything exists. It is beyond human capacity or even imagination even to begin to conceive of what that God must be like. He is beyond our sight and beyond all comprehension. And in the passage from John's Gospel we see Philip the disciple wrestling with this very problem. 'Show me the Father and I will believe you.'

Jesus' reply addresses the very centre of Christian faith. Jesus is God, but present to us in human form. Perfectly human yet perfectly divine. 'Whoever has seen me has seen the Father' Jesus reassures his disciples:

**Jesus said that 'If you know me, you will know my Father also. From now on you do know him and have seen him.'**

**Philip said to him, 'Lord, show us the Father, and we will be satisfied.'**

**Jesus said to him, "Have I been with you all this time, Philip, and you still do not know me? Whoever has seen me has seen the Father! How can you say? 'Show us the**

Father?' Do you not believe that I am in the Father and the Father is in me? The words that I say to you I do not speak on my own; but the Father who dwells in me does his works. Believe me that I am in the Father and the Father is in me."

(John—chapter 14, verses 7–11)

Knowing that, like us, his congregation can find the nature of God the Father and his relationship to Jesus the Son mystifying, Saint Paul puts his explanation into words that are simple and unmistakable:

'He is the image of the invisible God… for in him all the fullness of God was pleased to dwell.' (Letter to the Colossians, chapter 1, verses 15 and 19)

All the fullness of God. In the human form of Jesus. Accessible and comprehensible. With us and for us. Through Him the nature of God the Father is a source of wonderment, not just of wondering. And we are invited to approach the Father through Jesus and in the power of the Holy Spirit, every time we pray. As we do together now:

Heavenly Father, mystery beyond all comprehending, love beyond all understanding. We come to you in prayer, from our loneliness and need, as your dear Son Lord Jesus has taught us to do. Confident that you will hear our prayer. And that our cry will come unto you.

Amen.

# 30. A Revolutionary Way of Living

One of the most important moments in Luke's Gospel is the time when Jesus describes what it means to follow him. These so-called 'Beatitudes' (Blessings or Blessedness) are often mistaken for a command to suffer in silence in the hope of Heaven. 'Pie in the sky when you die', as this attitude is often unkindly called. In fact, nothing could be further from the truth of what Jesus is saying. He is giving his hearers back then (and us today) a rallying cry, an invitation to overturn the expected by being and behaving in a way that is totally revolutionary. To stand for the complete opposite of the habits of society at large, then and indeed now!

**Then he looked up at his disciples and said:**

**'Blessed are you who are poor, for yours is the kingdom of God. Blessed are you who are hungry now, for you will be filled.'**

**'Blessed are you who weep now, for you will laugh.'**

**'Blessed are you when people hate you, and when they exclude you, revile you, and defame you on account of the Son of Man. Rejoice on that day and leap for joy, for surely your reward is great in Heaven; for that is what their ancestors did to the prophets.'**

'But woe to you who are rich, for you have received your consolation.'

'Woe to you who are full now,

for you will be hungry.

'Woe to you who are laughing now, for you will mourn and weep.'

'Woe to you when all speak well of you, for that is what their ancestors did to the false prophets.'

'But I say to you that listen, love your enemies, do good to those who hate you, bless those who curse you, pray for those who abuse you. If anyone strikes you on the cheek, offer the other also; and from anyone who takes away your coat do not withhold even your shirt. Give to everyone who begs from you; and if anyone takes away your goods, do not ask for them again. Do to others as you would have them do to you.'

These words of Jesus would have sounded like outrageous revolution to the people who listened. They and he lived in a society that was ruled in a way in which success, outward show, competitive striving and neglect of others was the norm. (Which suggests that we haven't changed very much over the last two thousand years!) The only way to break the iron grip of this poisonous way of behaving is to be different says Jesus. To confront hate with love, selfishness with compassion and understanding of other people. To replace arrogance with humility. That way, and only that way, says Jesus we can change society. By living what we believe, and demonstrating that God's way is greater than the world's way.

Every little act of kindness and love, every concern for the greater good, they all help to signal the coming of God's

Kingdom. In whatever way we can, quietly more often than dramatically, we are all called to be witnesses to this better way. That's what it means, says Jesus, to be my follower. So although we may be apart, let us pray together for the coming of God's Kingdom and our part in the change that is needed.

**Heavenly Father, who showed us, through the ministry, death, and Resurrection of your beloved Son, what you planned for the world to be and how we can help to make it happen, strengthen our resolve to be faithful followers of Jesus' way, so that all that we think or do or say may be not for the world's vanity but for your glory. And for the building up of your Kingdom here on Earth.**

**Amen.**

# 31.'Oh for a Closer Walk With God'

*'O for a closer walk with God,*
*a calm and heavenly frame,*
*a light to shine upon the road*
*that leads me to the lamb!'*

That beautiful old hymn sings of the Christian journey of faith on which we follow where Jesus leads. I find it both inspiring and challenging every time I join in with the singing. And at no time is the inspiration from this hymn more strong or the challenge more obvious than now as we draw near to Holy Week. When Jesus' own walk of faith leads him to Calvary, to shameful Crucifixion but then beyond the pain to joyful Resurrection.

It's a journey of two kinds of love. His for us, who offered himself as loving sacrifice. And for us, it is a time to return that love and commitment, as we do our best to walk faithfully with him in our hearts along the rocky road that he volunteered to travel for our salvation. And then to share with him the promise of Resurrection, and the joy that outweighs all pain. It's such a powerful promise of freedom at this time of the lockdown that imprisons us, a time when our own road can seem so dark and steep!

The 'closer walk' that the hymn writer William Cowper longs for is what we most crave for on our own walk of faith. To know the closeness of Christ in our lives. And as we embark on that salvation journey the tragedy and the triumph of the Easter story are mingled until the pain of Good Friday gives way to the triumph that wins out so gloriously on Easter Sunday.

Next time I write to you it will be time for us to celebrate that triumph together in spirit, although many of us may still be physically apart. Meanwhile, may God keep every one of you safe and strong and give us all 'a light to shine upon the road that leads us to the Lamb'.

**Heavenly Father, shine on our road, strengthen our faith, fill us with hope, as the Easter story gives us yet again the promise of your loving care for us. Walk with us today Lord, and guide us each day along the road to our destination in your eternal presence.**

**Through Jesus Christ our Lord, the One who walks with us on every step of our journey of faith.**

**Amen.**

# 32. Never Give Up Hope

We all know what it is like to hope for something. For relief from pain or grief, loneliness or fear. For the return of happiness. Or simply for a change that in some way would alter our lives for good. And we know what it feels like to wait and wait for what seems like an eternity. The sad result is that so often we give up hope, lose our sense of trust. In ourselves, in life itself, and most sadly of all, in the love and care of God for us.

The passage here from John's Gospel is an object lesson in what it means to hope against the odds. And it tells us a lot about the way God looks out for and looks after all people, often against all appearances. Jesus is in Jerusalem for an important religious festival and he sees the group of invalids who congregate each day by the sacred pool of Beth-zatha, in the hope of being cured. And his compassion is aroused by the plight of one man in particular. We can imagine and even identify with the desperation he feels after 38 years of illness, and his despair at being elbowed out of the way day after day by supplicants who are faster than he is, as he can only crawl. He never makes it to the healing waters, and perhaps he never will.

But in one swift act of compassion Jesus heals the man and gives him his life and his freedom back. Although it is against Jewish law to do such things on the Sabbath, and this will be held against him later:

**After this there was a festival of the Jews, and Jesus went up to Jerusalem. Now in Jerusalem by the Sheep Gate there is a pool, called in Hebrew Beth-zatha, which has five porticoes. In these lay many invalids—blind, lame, and paralysed. One man was there who had been ill for 38 years. When Jesus saw him lying there and knew that he had been there a long time, he said to him, 'Do you want to be made well?'**

**The sick man answered him, 'Sir, I have no one to put me into the pool when the water is stirred up; and while I am making my way, someone else steps down ahead of me.' Jesus said to him, 'Stand up, take your mat and walk.' At once the man was made well, and he took up his mat and began to walk.**

**Now that day was a sabbath. So the Jews said to the man who had been cured, 'It is the sabbath; it is not lawful for you to carry your mat.'**

**But he answered them, The man who made me well said to me, "Take up your mat and walk."**

Our Christian religion is about faith, hope, and love, as St Paul tells us. And we need never give up. We can hold onto hope if we maintain our faith in the loving care of God, who often works in hidden and mysterious ways, ways that we may not understand, but always for love of us:

**Heavenly Father, with you all things are possible, for you have shown us what love looks like in the person of**

your beloved Son Jesus Christ. Strengthen our faith and hope that in the end all shall be well with us, however things may seem today. Through the love that created us and sustains us through our earthly life, and onwards into eternity.

Amen.

# 33. 'The Still Small Voice That Calls Us Home'

People often confess that the times—perhaps the only times—that they feel the presence of God, even sometimes actually hear God's voice, is at moments of greatest need. And we all know what those moments are like! This presence is usually not dramatic people say, more like a gentle whisper. So quiet it's hardly registered. And yet something changes profoundly for us because of God's gentle intervention.

In the reading below the prophet Elijah is in a state of exhausted despair. Fleeing from the wrathful revenge of Queen Jezabel who has vowed to kill him, he is hiding by cowering in a cave. Elijah has given up, doesn't know where to turn. And now he hears the voice of God, not in the dramatic way he might have expected, but in a gentle silence, not even a whisper:

**God said, 'Go out and stand on the mountain before the Lord, for the Lord is about to pass by'. Now there was a great wind, so strong that it was splitting mountains and breaking rocks in pieces before the Lord, but the Lord was not in the wind; and after the wind an earthquake, but the Lord was not in the earthquake; and after the earthquake**

a fire, but the Lord was not in the fire; and after the fire a sound of sheer silence. (1 King – chapter 19, verses 11–12)

When life seems to push us to the very edge of what we can cope with, we too may hear that 'sound of sheer silence', if we listen for it. The voice of reassurance from the God whose care and compassion for us is endless. And like Elijah we will be encouraged and renewed.

In the poem below I've tried to describe how we may listen and react to that still small voice that calls us to put our trust in God who is our home and our safe haven in the trials of life. This is my prayer for you and me, and for all of us.

Elijah heard the crashing of the thunder
He felt the earthquake saw the blinding light
But God was not in any of these wonders
Inside the cave that was as dark as night.
Until within the echoing of silence

There came a still small voice he'd always known
The voice that through the ages has pursued us
To bring us back, to call us to our home.

Instead of hearing Him inside ourselves
Are we too seeking God in the wrong place?
Are our impatient wanderings leading us
Away from recognising inward Grace?

And so like wanderers we hide and roam.
Until that still small voice calls us back home.

That home is like no other place.
It has no state but inward Grace
Like a dear lover in the night.
It comes to us and finds us out.

And it will find us, you and I,
Although we hide, although we fly
To hear or not is our free choice
When we are called by that sweet voice.
Amen.

# My Greatest Wish for You

I pray that you may always feel God's presence surrounding you, hear his gentle voice within you. Knowing that, whatever life may throw at you, you will always be 'unforgotten' and forever safe in God's loving hands. And I hope above all that in some small way this book may have helped you to strengthen and renew that faith and trust.